HALF PAST FIVE

V. ARORA

BlueRose Publishers

First Published in December 2020

ISBN: 978-93-5427-260-8

BLUEROSE PUBLISHERS

www.bluerosepublishers.com

info@bluerosepublishers.com

+91 8882 898 898

Cover Design:

Sanya Rastogi

Typographic Design:

Tanya Raj Upadhyay

Distributed by: BlueRose, Amazon, Flipkart, Shopclues

Please try to read it slow

I am for all reasons,

I am for all seasons.

1

Breathtakingly beautiful.
Dynamite of love, kindness,
and laughter.

The magic in her eyes
thrills me to die.
Her presence
questions my own existence.

I ask you, Divine Woman,
'Are you a child of God or God in disguise?'

2

REGRET IS THE BEST DECISION

It doesn't matter what I do
or what I choose.
The grass is always green
on the sides I have never seen.

3

BILLET-DOUX

It's been four days of our separation, my love,
and pieces of you have started leaving me.
Mornings are not the same
as they were before.
I sleep peacefully,
with an empty heart.
I don't want this;
I want you.
I want those sleepless nights
I've spent thinking of you,
thinking of us.

Without you,
I am simply a person.
An ordinary person,
busy with work and self-empowerment.
Please come back, my love,
and rekindle my soul.
Please come back,
your presence alone is enough for me.

And, you know,
I need to behold you to feel alive.

4

The thread between life and death
is thin,
broken in a snap,
taking away the precious ones.
All that is left are memories
or things left unsaid
or things we wish we shouldn't have said.

In the moment of our loss,
death becomes an alchemist,
turning the one who is gone
into a precious one.

Maybe all he wanted was
to be treated as precious while he was alive.

5

COURAGE

I saw a girl who couldn't see,
walking alone with an attentive glee.
Using a stick to trace her path,
counting the steps in her heart.

The road was busy with so much noise.
She chose to walk; she had no choice.
I was scared but wasn't she.
An ounce of fear I couldn't see.

I wanted to help but didn't do.
Nobody wants sympathy as they can do.
I watched her carefully as she walked.
She reached the bus and boarded the pass.

I walked back home with courage in my heart,
thinking all the way to make a new start.

6

I WISH

I wish life were easy,
like water flowing down a hill.
I wish life were a dream,
beautiful and serene.

But, sadly, it is not.
The road is marred with thorns,
of which I am born.

I wish I were rich,
a Cadillac and a mansion.
Life a bed of roses
and hard work an exemption.

7

PERFECTION

Perfection is what I seek,
to punish myself
for who I am not.

Perfection is what I seek,
to distract myself
from who I am.

Perfection is what I seek,
to fill the void between
me and my imaginary self.

8

DISSATISFACTION

Treat me the way
I want you to,
but I won't tell you how!

Love me the way
I want you to,
but I won't tell you how!

Read my mind,
read what I want
and when I want.

If you don't fulfill
my expectations,
feel my dissatisfaction.

9

I LOVE YOU

Sitting on my desk,
with hands pressed on a paper,
thinking what to write.

Your thoughts
come in a rush,
flooding me.
To write them or not
is not a choice,
but an urge
to which
I surrendered
and wrote three words in black ink:
'I love you'.

10

Sometimes, I get tired
of loving, caring, and worrying
for others.

Sometimes, I am so lost
in their dreams and pain
that I forget myself.

Sometimes, I just need
love, compassion, and respect.
Not from others,
but from myself.

11

EMPTY

I tried to write something for you, but nothing comes
to my mind. Feelings, tears, and thoughts all
have forsaken me.
I keep staring at the
blank paper.
I don't remember you.
I don't **EMPTY** remember
your face.
Who are you?
Suddenly, a tear rushed.
I stopped to feel it.
But, it dried.
This is my life without you,
my
love

12

CRUCIFIXION

You stood still at your beating.
You stood still when we were mocking.
Blessed us when we cursed you.
Kissed us when we hurt you.
We looked at you for our salvation
but did nothing at your crucifixion.
Why, Jesus, why?
Why did you suffer for our sins?
While we were showing our grins.

13

Comprehending my existence,
my afflictions, and my honour.
Hiding my deeds
in the ocean of love.
Ennobled by darkness
and lofty paradise.
Consoled by the tender
silk of death and
echo of longing.

14

SONG OF DESPAIR

Lord, why is the life of a rich man easy
and filled with abundance?
While the life of a poor man is
filled with despair and pain.
A rich man is always loved
and is forgiven for his sins.
Who will love and forgive a poor man?
The one who has nothing to give to anyone but love.
You were born in the house of a shepherd, Lord!
You gave them wisdom.
You gave them love.
But why didn't you give them wealth?

15

Truth bespeaks itself,
without the need of a speaker.
Language,
unscrutinised
yet simple and sweet.
Virtues, glories,
secrets, and sins–
all are treated equally.
For the purpose
is to reveal itself and
free the speaker.

It must be received carefully.
Don't rush
to find the meaning.
Carry it in your heart
as your own burden.
Surrender to God
by revealing it to him, and
you are free.

16

JUDGEMENT

We judge people,
as if
we have lived their lives.
Label them,
but hate to be labeled.
Limit the character of a person
to merely a definition,
a category.

Why is it difficult to see
the loveliness of others
when we are angry?
Why do we judge people?
When will I learn?
When will we all learn
that everything around us
exists for its own sake?

17

What to pursue?
Reality
or dreams?
How should one act?
To act or not to act?
Trapped in the illusion
of life,
of self.

Separating ourselves from God
and from our actions.
Renunciation of path
doesn't bring bliss
but utmost faith and meditation
of self and God within.

18

DEJECTION

Fighting does no good;
words hurled hurt equally
as a gunshot.
One marks the beginning of suffering
and other the end.

To fight back is to
start a battle with so much
blood and heartbreaks.
To sit silent isn't wise.

What to do
to end the suffering
without hurting anyone?
It is not possible,
and I feel dejected
with my inability.

19

A SIGN

Yesterday,
I asked God
for a sign.
To guide me
and tell me
I'm worthy.
I asked God
to make it rain.
I asked for the rain
in the middle of the winter,
and it is raining now.

20

Walking on my path,
I saw a light
shining so bright.
I wondered if it was a distraction
or a reward for my journey so far?
I was confused.
I followed the light and
left my path.
Now I hate myself
for yielding to the light,
but I think I would have hated myself
even after rejecting the light.

21

DEVOTION

I asked myself,
'What is devotion?'
'Is it a form of love?'
I started reading poems.
I could find
longing, pain,
joy, and ecstasy,
but devotion was not there.

I started reading scriptures,
the Holy books.
I found one;
I read about his life and
his devotion to his beloved.
Since then I've been fasting
every Tuesday.

22

SACRIFICE

To put others first.
To treat their needs
as our own needs.

Is it a sacrifice?

To kill an innocent animal
to please the God.
To kill more
if God is not pleased.

Is it a sacrifice?

An action without an intention–
Is it possible?
Is it a sacrifice?

Can we be free from our intentions?
What if we have an intention,
but we are not aware of it?

What is this sacrifice?
Is it real?

Jesus died for us.
He sacrificed himself for us,
but he was aware of his intentions.
Are we?

23

TO LIVE OR NOT TO LIVE

'To live or not to live?'
I asked myself.

Weighing each side,
unbalanced, I stumbled.

To live or not to live?

On one side is life,
with its joy and afflictions.
On the other side is death,
with its unreal reality,
a place
I know nothing about.

I am at a crossroad.
I have two choices–
To embrace or to let go.
I am confused–
To embrace death or my afflictions?

I cheated death, and
it still haunts me.

24

Walking alone
on a cold morning,
with empty streets
and your thoughts in my mind.
Why can't I stop thinking of you?
Why are you present everywhere?
The words I speak
carry your essence.
I am not myself anymore!
Your every action seems to me a gift.
Why do I understand them so easily?
I spend hours reflecting on my actions,
but I don't have to spend even a minute reflecting on yours.
Can you tell me what is happening to me?

25

MISTAKES

To do it or not,
I often contemplated.

One day I did it
and failed.
Lost everything I had.

Embraced by insecurity
and nothing to hold on,
I gave up and sat in despair,
thinking about what I have lost
and the lessons I have learned.
It seemed to me,
I have gained more in my loss.

26

I AM GUILTY

I am guilty
of doubting your love,
of doubting my strength.

I am guilty
of giving up on you
even for a moment,
and that moment
changed everything.

I am guilty
of accepting my temperaments
but not accepting myself.

I am guilty
of acting wise
and speaking like a fool.

Now I am drowning in the ocean of my guilt,
with the hope that you will come and save me.

27

Your words
carry your essence.
I live by them,
I live with them.

To make me feel humble
and accept them
as a gift of love and pain,
as a truth about you and me.
To remember them
is not a choice
but a need, and
I remember them with my heart.

28

LIFE OF A ROSE

I was young, so was the love.
Embraced by light, I took a big flight.
I opened my petals to feel the love,
the intimate moments and the passion above.

Love was abundant; I opened up more.
And then I started drifting to the shore.
Life became heavy; I needed support.
And they tied me to a rope.

Alas! One day came the rain.
Took away all the beauty and gave me the pain.
Everything was lost from up and down.
Petals of love started to fall on the ground.

29

BUFFER

The joys of life
and all its afflictions.
All my failures
and all my convictions.
My need for someone
or something
to take me out of this mess.
And music acts as a buffer in my life.

30

IF WE LOVE EACH OTHER MORE

If we love each other more
        when we are not lovable.
If we love each other more
        when we are in trouble.
If we love each other more
        when we remember our past.
If we love each other more
        when we doubt if it will last.
It could have worked
        if we loved each other more.
It could still work
        if we love each other more.

31

BLOOM NO MORE, YOUNG BUD, BLOOM NO MORE

Bloom no more, young bud, bloom no more.
For you'll be taken away from your source.
You'll fill their home with your exotic smell
and beautify everything, even the burning hell.

You'll get nothing in return for this sacrifice.
Longing for the sun, alone you'll die.
What you'll do with your wasted existence?
They won't care for your love and persistence.
No one will mourn when you'll die, and
you'll be replaced with another life.

Young bud:

What should I do if I don't bloom?
Live a life of fear and gloom?
I'm a flower, a symbol of love, and
you, my friend, want me to hate?
The gardens are beautiful due to my presence.
Let hell be beautiful too, for it is always abandoned.

Don't forget, love is all about giving,
no matter how difficult and how short is living!

32

IN MY SECRET LIFE

In my secret life,
the stars always shine so bright, and
the moon glows in the broad daylight.
There is only joy and delight.
But only in my secret life.

I laugh at the sufferings of life
and fight my battles without any strife.
There are no truths and lies.
Neither Shiva nor Christ.
These are few things I have.
But only in my secret life.

33

BETTER LUCK NEXT TIME!

On my knees,
holding the ring:
'Will you marry me?'
You said, 'Yes', but
the ring could not fit.

34

SONG OF LIFE

If today is my end,
    I'll die with a tear and a smile.
If today is my new beginning,
    I'll live with a tear and a smile.
Anything that touches my soul
    leaves me breathless, perplexed,
    and questions my existence.
And I'm here with my arms opened,
    whirling to the song of life.

35

CHEERS

Cheers to the battles I haven't yet fought.
Cheers to the battles I've lost.
Cheers to the sun for shining on me.
Cheers to the night for sheltering me.
Cheers to the womb in which I was born.
Cheers to the world I am from.
Cheers to every forgotten soul.
Cheers to everything my heart could hold.

36

DELIRIUM

Freed from the cage
of memories
and mistakes.

Enshrouded by imagination
of how things should be!

A moment of bliss
followed by
moments of melancholy.

Another cage?
Scouring and suffocating!

Crawling and bleeding
for freedom
which doesn't exist.

37

I AM NOT A CYNIC

I–trust
A–nd it is always broken.
M–akes me wonder. But
N–O
O–ffence
T–aken.
A–lways free but not for sale.
C–ollaging
Y–our
N–egligence to
I–nflame my
C–anvas.

38

DEAR MOM

Dear Mom,
I am aware of things
you do for me
and do not do
for yourself.

Your sacrifices are not unheeded.
I feel them in my bones.

I can feel those nine months
I've spent in your womb
and those sleepless nights
you spent to nurse me.

But, Mom,
I can never feel what
it is like being a mother.
I can never feel that.

I will never know
from where you harness
this strength,
this never-ending love.

I will never know.

I know you've been
asking me all along
for one thing–my happiness.
I promise,
I will be happy.

39

FOREVER

Sun shines perpetually,
day and night,
summers and winters.

Earth changes
the axis,
endearing and separating.
The sun shines
through clouds and rain.

This is the love
I have for you, my beloved.

Forever.

40

TO FEEL YOU

I know the pain of speaking too much
and not speaking at all.
One takes me higher,
and the other lets me fall.
Which one is good?
I don't know!
I really don't know!

In between the silence and too much talking,
there is a field.
No one meets there.

Fear,
passion,
and longing
stir my soul,
and I am not myself.

Losing myself
to feel you.

To feel you.

41

Success alludes me,
for it wants a higher price.
But I have not yet failed 10,000 times,
to give up.

42

Unprepared,
but I am aware
of the good times waiting for me
on the other side of the tunnel.

43

Yesterday I was ignorant.
Today I am ignorant too,
but I know.

44

SHE DOESN'T KNOW

She doesn't know
how much I love her,
how much I die to see her smile.

She doesn't know
if I am okay,
because I pretend to be.

The breeze is warm and cold at the same time.

She doesn't know
I'm always fighting two battles.
One for myself and
the other for her.

45

An unidentified dead body.
A woman who sold her soul and is now dead.
A girl who was raped and killed.
A soldier who was killed in a battle
or was waiting for it.
A battle lost to cancer or depression–
They didn't want to die.
There is no bravery and glory in death.
No art will make their death beautiful, and
they won't speak from their graves.

If you care,
support their family and loved ones.
Sacrifice your dreams, your time,
and your money for them.

46

I have no expectations
from you
or the universe.
Because I have been given
what I want
and what I do not want.

47

Is it worth being good?

Goodness does
nothing
good
to the good people.

48

SAD TUNES

If there is no pain,
there won't be any music.
If there is no music,
what will you sing when you're happy?

49

Working
to become someone else
and lose myself
in the crowd.

50

I LONG TO SPEND MY LIFE ON A PLACE LIKE THIS

5,000 meters above the sea.
No trains, no cars, only human feet.
Where connections are cherished,
as they are rare.
Where weed is a weed as it is everywhere.
Where everything is holy from breath to kiss.
Where else on earth could I find
the eternal bliss?
A place where I am one with nature,
no ego, no jealousy, as she is my teacher.

51

FINGERS

Index: Contending and accusing others to free ourselves from guilt.
Middle: To free ourselves from the cage of emotions.
Ring: Anulus pronubis, a symbol of eternal love.
Little: Pinky promise, making promises we might not keep.

And if you want a thumb: keep it up.

52

WATER

Bottle of whisky
sucks emotional heaven,
distilling maelstrom.

53

YOU BURN

Life isn't always about being successful
or being on the top of the world
or healing every broken soul you meet.

Sometimes, it's about loving someone or
being loved.
Sometimes, it's about staying in darkness and
staying there forever.
Sometimes, all you have is money and
sometimes only love.

No matter what your purpose of life is, YOU BURN.
You burn from passion,
desires, and
hate.
You burn.
Everything that lives, burns.

54

KILLER

Some kill themselves; we call it suicide.
Some kill out of frustration, for they can't abide.
I kill not, but yet I kill
all the emotions inside me.
I, too, am a killer.

55

WALK ALONE

When

All you can

re**L**ate to is the loneliness of

the s**K**y, for it is

Always

e**L**usive to

Our eyes,

a**N**d they have an

Excuse for being small.

56

DEATH

Life becomes **D**reary when
loneliness **E**ngulfs the soul,
which once was **A**live
with the hope of **T**omorrow.
Helium.

57

A TRAGIC TALE

She stood there,
silent and motionless,
like a work of art.

He stood there,
silent and struggling
to bring her back to life.

She couldn't be moved,
and he couldn't move.

He stood there
fighting for her,
and time played it's cards.

He is still there
in his grave.
She is also there,
motionless,
waiting to be rescued.

Some stories end tragically, and
some are tragic.

58

THERE IS ALWAYS A WAY

There is a way to get things done.
There is a way to work in the sun.
There is a way to touch the stars.
There is a way to heal our scars.
There is a way to clean the dust.
There is a way we can build trust.
There is a way to make it last.
There is a way slow and fast.

There is always a way.

59

WHEN IT RAINS

The bursting clouds
and the striking light
force the birds
to abandon the flight.

But there is a bird,
who rejoices in rain,
singing the song of love and pain.

60

THE LETTER

SpatTered
witH
firE,

the fLaring
hEart
Tells
litTle
ovEr
papeR.

BeneaTh
tHe
leavEs,

Loveliness
squeEzing
Through
uncerTain
tirEd
viRgin.

Moon**L**ight

draggl**E**d

agains**T**

smoo**T**h,

bar**E**

inkd**R**ops.

61

Love is left on the mercy of fate.
Alone it stands waiting for grace.
Once a melodious song but now
it is shuddering in the dungeon of silence
and screaming for life.
Love is left on the mercy of the rain,
with a river flowing nearby.

62

NOT ALL FLOWERS BLOOM

I grew up in a lab,
ether and pyridine,
HeLa and MCF-7,
laser and prism.

I grew up in a gym,
biceps and triceps,
shoulder, back, and thighs,
inner and outer.

I grew up in my room,
among books and songs,
creativity and arts,
happiness and life.

I grew up in heartache
and mind trained to pain.
I grew up in a field,
with no loss no gain.

I grew up in an illusion
of hope and despair.
I grew up thinking
someone should be there.

I grew up traveling
four hours a day.
I grew up waiting
all night and all day.

63

SOLITUDE

I've found a place to sit
on a mountain partially covered with snow.
I don't know how far I can see;
the world is as big as your heart is.
My eyes know every place in your heart.

Eagles are looking for their prey.
They can have a part of me;
I don't mind!

I'll leave you
and your thoughts here.

64

Fire was lit to burn an incense.
Instead, a thought sparked in my mind.
It is about you.
It is always about you,
but I know you don't care.

Life seems to be flowing like a river.
I really don't know where I will end up.
Maybe the journey hasn't started yet!

People have left, because
they got what they'd wanted.
I'm staying, because
I never asked for anything.
I'll wait for the moon
to light up the river.
I need your light!
I always needed you.
But you left me
for the one who waited for you.

My feet is cold,
but my heart isn't.
Can I pledge to keep myself clean?
But from what?
This loneliness!
I can't!
I need it more than I need you.
That's why I should give it up.

I'll go back to hotel
and find some friends.

65

The
only
difference
between
good
and
bad
is
love.

66

A good character
is better than
a thousand prayers
in shaping your destiny.

67

Your beauty died the day
you wore your
nail-fitted shoes and
walked over the tender grounds
just to survive.

68

Somewhere in my heart,
there will always be a person
I could not be.

69

CHOOSE ONE EACH DAY

Unprejudiced objectivity.

Integrity.

Striving for excellence.

Compassion.

Inquisitiveness.

Respect.

Eloquence.

Persuasiveness.

Discipline.

Thoroughness.

Conscience.

Inspiration.

Health-consciousness.

Over-generosity.

Content.

Adventure.

Vision.

70

HATE-PRAYER

May the people who always try to prove others wrong
be wrong in every decision of their lives.
May the people who mock others for their insecurities
be robbed of all the securities they have.
May the people who treat others as their doormats
be robbed of their homes where their hearts feel comfortable.
May the people who pretend to be in trouble for seeking attention
and mock the person helping them lose their mind.
May the people who only believe in taking
lose their possessions, for the very essence of humanity is sharing.
May the people who feel strong by pushing others down
be weak in their immune systems.
May the people who use others and discard them when they are done
be useless to themselves.

71

Why are you so hideous of your possessions?
Why do you believe only in taking?
And why don't you share with others?
Remember, if all you want is only for yourself,
one day karma will knock at your door, and
you'll have so much to give.